THE WONDERFUL FATHER BOOK

Turnbull & Willoughby
Publishers

THE WONDERFUL FATHER BOOK

Richard Mann
Illustrated by Todd Doney

First printing March 1985

10   9   8   7   6   5   4   3   2   1

Manufactured in the United States of America

Published by Turnbull & Willoughby Publishers, Inc.
1151 West Webster
Chicago, IL 60614

ISBN: 0-943084-23-7

Library of Congress Catalog Number 84-052460

Photography by Art Wise Studio
Illustrations by Todd Doney
Wonderful father photos of Scott Doney

Dedication

When I was performing in the circus as a clown, a father came up to me, slipped me a ten dollar bill and asked if I would do a little trick for his son, something like taking off my thumb.

I was a bit confused. Ten dollars seemed like a lot to pay for a simple stunt like that. I asked him why he didn't do it himself. "Aw," he sighed, "it never works for me. The kid doesn't get it."

So, years later, for that father and his son, I dedicate this book.

Author with 3 day old daughter
Eve Madelaine (In a top hat
already!)

Table of Laughs & Giggles

Goofing Off

Silly clown business

Hand Jive

Tricks with hands

Cashing In

Tricks with money

Shhhh . . .

Silent bits

Face to Face

The art of making funny mugs

Introduction

I love to make them laugh . . .

Kids are great. They never cease to amaze me with their inexhaustible energy, unlimited imagination and, most of all, their wonderfully un-inhibited sense of humor.

Kids love to laugh and I love to make them laugh.

They are so energetic and imaginative, it's important to hold their attention long enough to complete a trick or stunt.

Working with children for many years as a clown, as a magician and now as a father has taught me that it's not so much the trick that delights your audience; it's more in the way the trick is done.

Out of this realization came *The Wonderful Father Book.*

I found that telling a funny story or adding an extra bit of silliness can make all the difference. I call this element the *Old Razzle-Dazzle,* and it's probably the most important part of every trick in this book.

The tricks themselves have been around forever as part of the repertoire of countless fathers, uncles and brothers.

None of these tricks is difficult. In fact, they are so easy that they don't require any skill, but they can make your child — and maybe a few grownups — laugh and giggle. And more important, they can help you discover new, fun time to spend together with your family.

It's a good idea to keep this book away from your kids. After all, why should they have all the fun playing jokes on you? If they ever discover how simple some of this trickery is, you might not seem quite so amazing!

You should read through each trick before trying it out. Some of the stunts are easy enough to be done with little or no practice, but you should become familiar with them so that you don't stumble through the steps.

You can use the razzle-dazzle as it's written, although I strongly recommend that you use my material as a springboard for your own imagination. By all means, use any anecdote or twist you can dream up. Remember, this is your moment to shine for your kids. Develop your own style and your kids will love it.

Keep your patter light and fanciful. Throw in a couple of wild claims to entice and hold their interest. Keep it fun.

By taking advantage of my tips about *The Old Razzle-Dazzle* you can avoid the possibility of the kids looking blankly at you and saying, "So, what happened?" or "Boy, Pop, that was pretty dumb." You can be much more confident that you will have a happy audience.

Try doing one of these tricks without any set-up or patter and watch how fast it falls flat. Despite your good intentions, if you kept this up your children would suddenly find all sorts of excuses not to watch. (Of course, that would be one way to get them to do their homework or clean their rooms!)

Remember that some of the tricks can best be described as *very* silly. Their intention is to coax a groan as well as a laugh. The whole idea is to

have fun. I have included them because kids love to discover you have done a trick even *they* could do.

Think silly, think ridiculous . . . or, better yet, think clown.

You might change your expression, muss your hair, cock your hat, walk funny, change your voice or just cross your eyes. Try to give your act a different character. I become "The Great Dadd-O," a pompous, comical remembrance of my circus days.

Don't be afraid to make mistakes because they are bound to happen. Accept your flub graciously and turn it all into a good-natured joke. Kids love finding you out. I know it was always a relief for me to know that my dad was slightly less than perfect.

There's no guarantee this material will win you a spot on a late-night talk show or in a Vegas revue, but it's all time-tested and sure to win the hearts of the few who really count — the children. And best of all, it's guaranteed to make you the "star" of the family.

So have fun and enjoy the laughter.

R. Mann

change m
the circu
audien
atio
y

Important points to remember before your debut . . .

If the stunts in this book are so simple, why do they work marvelously for Uncle Buddy while eliciting little more than confused stares when you attempt them? It can't be brains — you're much smarter than he is. It can't be coordination — he can't walk and chew gum at the same time.

What *is* the difference?

The Daddy with Funny Stories!

I've seen many fathers and uncles perform simple tricks without any build-up or clever story and then scratch their heads in wonderment when the gags fall flat. "Gee," they say, "I saw Uncle Lee do it and everyone laughed. What's the magic?"

It's not magic or skill. It's razzle-dazzle. My professional experience as a clown taught me that every trick needs a build-up, whether it's a clever story, some funny expressions or maybe even a long silence to help build suspense. If you learn nothing else from this book, learn the importance of the *Old Razzle-Dazzle*. Once you understand how crucial it

is, you'll even be able to create your own silly tricks. *Who cares if they're astounding or not? With fun razzle-dazzle, the tricks will be fun too.*

And don't assume that *my* razzle-dazzle is the only one or the best one for you or your child. Analyze a trick and try to create a story that relates better to you or your child. I often

"patter" depending on
circumstances or the age of my
audience. Develop your own variations. And don't be afraid to make
your razzle-dazzle longer than I've
shown here.

Tears Turn to Smiles!

Here's a razzle-dazzle variation I use
often: The Personalized-Up-To-The-
Minute Razzle-Dazzle.

There is usually a specific reason
why a child is unhappy and needs
cheering up. Once you know the
reason, try to customize a razzle-
dazzle for that problem:

"Bob hit me again!" (Quick, which
tricks relate to strength? Karate
Potato? Money Bridge? Vanishing
Pencil?)

"I lost my lunch money!" (Hole in
Hand? Vanishing Quarter?)

When my friend Ralph's daughter
fell on the sidewalk and hurt her
hand, nothing could make her stop
crying. At least, nothing poor Ralph
could do. Enter Uncle Richard with a
personalized razzle-dazzle concern-
ing the time I fell on the sidewalk and
how I have a "hole in my hand" to
this day. (I ran to the first store I saw
and yelled, "A sheet of paper! Any
paper will do; my niece hurt her
hand. They looked at me very quiz-
zically since they didn't understand I
was only trying to get a prop so I
could be a Wonderful Uncle.)

Think of each trick by category and
you can create a razzle-dazzle to fit
almost any reason for unhappiness.
This is the time that razzle-dazzle is
needed most, and there's nothing
more heart-warming to a parent
than being able to turn tears or a
grumpy face into a big, bright smile.

Prepare for the Giggles!

I know I told you these are all easy
tricks, but please do me a favor and
read each one *completely* before
trying it. "Prepare for the giggles"
doesn't mean sitting back and waiting

13

for the applause. It means *prepare,* as in *practice.*

If you try a trick just once and then perform, at worst you'll flop and at best you'll be less than entertaining. Remember how clever children can be. Don't think you can fool or entertain them without "polishing your act." Practice, practice, practice until you are comfortable with each trick you want to perform.

"Ha, Ha, I Saw That!"

Sometimes you won't care if a trick flops because your intent was just to have some silly fun. But other times you may be trying to elicit some ooohs and aaahs of amazement and don't want to get "caught." This is the time to watch your "sight lines."

A sight line is the view that your *audience has of you* while you are performing. Remember to let the children see only what you want them to see. Unless you think about your sight lines, you risk hearing

cries of, "Ha, ha, I saw how you did that?" (See the Amazing Detachable Digit for a good illustration of when sight lines can be crucial.)

"Do it Again, Daddy!"

Okay, so they loved your act. Now you're getting delusions of grandeur. You start thinking you'd be a *real* big hit on the *Tonight Show* and you assume if "once is good, twice is better." Be careful!

That naive 4-year old you fooled the first time is *really* watching the second time and chances are he won't be fooled again. Remember, the first time your audience didn't know what to expect, but the second time your element of surprise is gone.

Here's where a little razzle-dazzle helps. Can you think of some clever reasons why you *can't* do a stunt the second time? You'd better or you won't be wonderful for very long.

Having Fun Together!

Last, but most important of all, remember to have *fun*. This book was written not only so you can make your children laugh and giggle, but so you can all laugh and giggle *together* — so you and your children can spend more fun time with each other.

When you get right down to it, how expertly you perform a trick isn't really important. (It may be in a circus with paying customers, but fathers have love on their side.) Whether you turn out to be a star or a flop as a performer of silly tricks, you can be sure that spending this kind of happy time together with your children is certainly a big part of being a Wonderful Father.

No Tricks

Tricks That
Do Themselves

What could be better than
these little wonders that do
all the work themselves and
you just take the bows?

Karate Potato

Driving a straw through a potato

The proper razzle-dazzle for this trick makes the effect marvelous. It was Uncle Cyril's performance of this simple stunt that first convinced me it *must* require more than human strength to master such an amazing feat.

Props:
One medium-sized (must be Idaho) potato and one plastic soda straw.

The Old How-To:

(1.) Hold the potato in your left hand with your palm to one side so the straw won't strike you when it pierces the potato. (2.) Hold the straw as shown, placing your index finger over the end of the straw. Grasping the potato firmly, start your stroke with the straw up near your face.

Stab the spud squarely, *making certain not to break the momentum of your swing*. (Don't *jab at the* spud; swing all the way through. Although this appears to be a feat of strength, it is actually the inertia that makes the trick work.)

The Old Razzle-Dazzle:

Without speaking, Uncle Cyril would hold the potato in his hand and gaze at it as if he were in a trance.

Finally, he would put the straw against the potato. Without breaking his gaze, he would slowly raise the straw. He'd pause, then lower the straw again.

Here he would pause again. Suddenly, taking a deep breath, he would quickly raise the straw and — yelling out "HEY-YAH!" like a karate expert — stab the potato. The effect was devastating!

This is one of those tricks in which the razzle-dazzle is silence and exaggerated concentration rather than a clever tale. Take it slowly and let your audience's curiosity and interest build.

Getting Clipped

Flipping paper clips from a dollar

More often than not, it's the simple little tricks, like this one, that hold the greatest fascination. Without a doubt, this stunt is the product of some bored executive who sat around his office with nothing to do, but children's eyes really light up when they see the outcome. Then they can't wait to try it.

Props: Two paper clips and a dollar bill.

The Old How-To:

(1) Bend the dollar into an S shape, as shown. (2) Place the paper clips so that each is clipping an outer and an inner edge of the S. (3) Pull the dollar from both ends in a horizontal line. The clips will fly off the bill and clip themselves to each other.

The Old Razzle-Dazzle:

Begin with the dollar bill already folded into an S. "Ladies and gentlemen, for the first time on this stage you are about to witness a daring display of skill and dexterity. Ladies and gentlemen, direct from the Five and Dime Circus and Stationery Store, the Dopey Duo." Introduce the two paper clips to the cheering crowd.

"The crowd is hushed as our two brave performers scale the sides of this dollar bill. Perched high above the arena floor, our courageous couple is about to attempt a spectacular feat." I usually "walk" them out to the stage like they are little people.

"On the count of three they will leap high into the air and come down holding hands." Take hold of both ends of the bill.

"May we have a drum roll, please? And now, one . . . two" — pull the ends of the dollar — "three . . . and the crowd goes wild!"

The clips, as promised, will fly into the air and come down joined.

The kids will no doubt want to try it immediately; you know how they are.

Once you have taught the kids how to do the trick, you might want to form teams and have a leaping paper clips Olympics, sort of an odd variation on pitching pennies.

Of course, avoid flipping the clips at anyone and discourage the children from shooting them at each other.

Born with a Silver Spoon

How to hang a spoon on the end of your schnoz

This particular bit of tom-foolery is a big favorite of my daughter Eve Madelaine. She is often kept amused with this stunt in restaurants while we wait for our dinner. It must seem odd when our waitress finally returns and finds dad, mom and even little Evie wearing our silverware on our noses.

Props: One lightweight metal teaspoon

The Old How-To:

The only secret is that your spoon should be slightly warm (body temperature will do).

(1) Start by using a napkin to wipe your nose and the teaspoon. This will remove any excess oil from the surfaces of both.

(2) Warm the spoon by clasping it tightly in your hands or by breathing on it.

(3) Tilt your head *slightly* and place the spoon on your nose. Adjust it a little until you feel it begin to "take hold." A little practice and this becomes simple. Remember, the spoon must be body temperature.

The Old Razzle-Dazzle:

The visual effect of this trick is enough; don't announce it.

I begin with a very dramatic and serious attitude. This adds to the mystery and the overall absurdity of what is about to happen. Once the spoon is in place, I might even cross my eyes and stick out my tongue. A class act!

At the finish, I pretend the spoon is stuck to my face. I tug and pull on the spoon until finally, it seems to "rip" free. This tickles the little funny bones.

Once you have mastered this primary effect, you might want to try a little experimenting. Try hanging more than one spoon at a time. After extensive training, I am able to hang eight teaspoons on various parts of my face, to the overwhelming delight of my little girl. A strange claim to fame.

The Impressive Press
Balancing a sheet of newspaper

I once knew a fellow who could balance just about anything on his chin. He used to amaze us by balancing a chair, a card table and even a ten-foot ladder. One day he told me he was going to balance a sheet of newspaper. I thought he was joking. He wasn't.

Props: One sheet from a *tabloid-sized* newspaper.

The Old How-To-Do:

(1) Hold the paper vertically by diagonal corners. Pull the sheet taut, firmly but gently so as not to tear it. (2) Pinch the corners, giving them a slight crease. This will give the sheet a sort of backbone. (3) Balance the paper by the lower corner resting on your finger tips.

The Old Razzle-Dazzle:

First, roll the paper into a tube, tape it and balance it on your fingers. Make it seem like a big deal. The kids will respond enthusiastically just to show you up.

Continue by rolling the sheet into a cone and balancing it. The kids will certainly jump at this second challenge. It's slightly more difficult, but I'm sure it won't take them long to master.

Finally, lay the paper flat. "Well, you didn't seem to have too much trouble with those. Let's see if you can balance this sheet of newspaper like this." Pick up the paper and hold it as if you are going to balance it, but don't.

Give the sheet to one of the kids and let him try. After he attempts it a few times, let someone else try it. Once they have seen how difficult it is to do, it's your turn.

Assume the position but let the paper go limp. This is to make them think that you can't do it, either. Some of the kids might even heckle you at this point.

"Now, be very quiet. It takes a lot of concentration to get the point of balance just right. There." Follow through this time with the balance and the kids just won't believe what they see.

Leave behind the paper flat and with the little creases smoothed out so they won't catch on too quickly.

The Reluctant Pop

Sticking a pin in a balloon without popping it.

It's a well known fact that children like noise, so this little stumper is a natural. Eve and her friend ZZ ask for this stunt quite often, and I have to laugh as they cover their ears and cringe before I have even inflated the balloon.

Props:

A few balloons, cellophane tape, large pin (straight pin, hat pin, etc.)

The Old How-To:

(1) Secretly prepare one balloon by blowing it up, knotting it and placing a small piece of tape on it.

(2) When the balloon is pierced through the center of the tape, it will not burst.

(3) Do not let go of the pin. This is to prevent the pin from flying in case of a premature pop.

The Old Razzle-Dazzle:

Tell the kids you have a question you want to ask them. Blow up and knot the balloon. Hold the balloon in one hand and the pin in the other. "What would happen if I stuck this balloon with this pin?" Pause.

Stick the balloon and pop it. This is just to get their attention. Now take out the second balloon, which you've secretly prepared with tape.

"They tell me that every time you stick a pin into a balloon, it will pop. But I don't agree that it happens all the time. Do you?" Ask one of the kids close by you and watch him cringe as you come near with the pin poised to strike.

"See, I think if you sneak up on the balloon and catch it off guard by slowly putting in the pin that it just won't know it's time to pop." Play with the kids at this point until you have them with their ears covered and giggling in anticipation of your theory being proved wrong.

Smugly push the pin into the balloon at the taped spot and watch their faces go from cringes to mouths wide open.

"You see, it works if you just sneak up on it. Here, you try it." Hand the pin to one of the children. (Put your finger over the hole to keep the air in.)

"Remember to move real slowly and be very quiet."

Coach your apprentice until the balloon meets with the pin. You'll scare the laughs right out of them.

Not Just Whistling Dixie
Making music with a straw

For such a simple little trick it creates quite a stir. You might want to carry a handful of straws for the kids and the adults because they will all want to try it. They will insist that you have a small "something" in your mouth that makes the shrill note but 'tis not so.

Props: One to a handful of plastic soda straws.

The Old How-To:

(1) Hold straw vertical in the right hand. Pinch the bottom of straw closed with the thumb and first finger. (2) Place top opening to lips. Blow across the opening as you would a pop bottle or a flute. (3) Once you have a note, pinch straw with left finger and thumb just above the right finger and thumb. Continue blowing as you slide the left fingers up the straw pinching it as you go. The pitch will rise to a very sharp whistle.

The Old Razzle-Dazzle:

Although the principal is very easy it requires some practice to get the sharp sound that grabs everyone's curiosity.

After dissecting the "How-to-do" of this stunt I have realized there are some definite tricks to the trick.

First, be sure to hold the straw pinched closed as you slide your fingers up. Second, get the right angle for the blow. Third, blow steady and hard. This will give you the clear crisp tone.

Fourth, don't tell anyone the first three pointers.

I carry wrapped soda straws with me so that I am always prepared. Never announce the trick, just do it. Sometimes everyone is caught off guard that no one sees who did it and look around to see who the smart aleck is.

It is quite a treat to watch the kids, and better, the adults trying their hand at this little gem. All of them think there has got to be a special trick. Most will resort to whistling over the straw trying to get that same sound.

This is perhaps the most requested of my repertoire.

Up In Smoke
Putting smoke inside bubbles

This small piece of wonder was probably invented by someone who couldn't quite get the hang of blowing smoke rings. It requires that you smoke a cigarette, but if you don't smoke, don't start for the sake of this stunt. You will be no less wonderful.

Props: A lit cigarette, a bottle of soap bubbles and a bubble blower.

The Old How-To:

(1) Take a good drag on the cigarette, but don't inhale. Hold the smoke in your mouth. (2) Dip the little wand into the soap solution and blow a bubble, exhaling the smoke as you do. The bubble will trap the swirling smoke inside and carry it away.

The Old Razzle-Dazzle:

Bubbles have always had a sort of hypnotizing effect on the young and old alike. No one can resist playing with them when I introduce a bottle of bubbles to a bunch of kids.

After the kids are caught up in chasing and popping the bubbles, I will blow a smoke bubble. I don't smoke, but I take a puff from someone's cigarette while no one is looking and hold the smoke in my mouth for a while before blowing the bubble.

Without fail, the kids and adults are audibly surprised as the mysterious bubble is formed and floats away. Everyone watches until the bubble finally pops and the smoke hovers for just a moment. It's almost like real magic.

For a special variation, try marrying a plain bubble with a smoke bubble as they're floating. It's pretty neat.

The Wavering Writer

A rubber pencil

This is an old optical illusion that still fascinates kids when they see it. In fact, don't be surprised if they grab the pencil away from you to make sure it isn't rubber. One little boy was convinced there was a hidden button you had to push to make the pencil wiggle like that.

Props: A wooden pencil or a pen, the longer the better.

The Old How-To:

(1) Hold the pencil *loosely* by its eraser between the thumb and first finger of your right hand, with your finger on top. The point of the pencil will hang slightly down. (2) Keeping your grip loose, move your hand and forearm up and down *quickly with short jerks*. This creates the illusion that the pencil has somehow turned into rubber. (3) Practice this a few times on your own to get the right movement of your hand and arm. After a while, you'll suddenly "get it" and the pencil will look so rubbery that you won't believe it yourself.

The Old Razzle-Dazzle:

Pick up the pencil as if you are about to write a note. Pretend you are having a hard time by wiggling the pencil as you try to write.

"There's something wrong here. I can't seem to get the pencil to write for me. Every time I try, it gets sort of limp. Here, see if it will write for you." Hand the pencil to one of the children.

"Well, it seems to be working all right now." Take back the pencil and begin to write once more. Again have it wiggle all over the paper. This will tickle the kids as you try to master the problem.

Hold the pencil up and begin shaking it. "I just don't get it. Look at that. How can anyone be expected to write with a rubber pencil?"

Shake it a bit more before tossing it onto the table. "They must have used real soft lead in that one."

Pick up another pencil and complete your note.

Oh Say Can You See . . ?

Making it look like there's a hole in your hand.

This optical illusion can really puzzle the kids. Their expressions are priceless when they first see the effect and then do a double take to make certain they saw what they saw.

The Old How-To:

(1.) Roll sheet of paper into a tube about an inch in diameter. (2.) With child's eyes closed, place your palm six inches from his left eye and the paper tube in front of the other eye. (3.) HAve the child open his eyes *slowly* and give them time to focus. It will appear as if he is looking through a hole in your palm. NOTE: Tell him to keep looking until his eyes begin to focus.

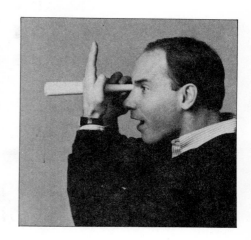

The Old Razzle-Dazzle:

This one requires a bit of a story for the lead-in. I tell the children about the time I found my first nickel:

"Well, I was so excited, I could hardly wait to spend it.

"My mother laughed and told me the nickel was going to burn a hole in my pocket. I certainly didn't want that to happen when I went to sleep that night so I held onto it very tightly.

"When I woke up the next morning, it was gone. I looked everywhere, but it was gone for sure. I think maybe that nickel had burned a hole right through my hand!

"Sometimes, when I look very closely, I can see light coming through my palm."

This sets up the illusion nicely. I then hold my hand up and ask the children if they can see the hole. Next, I choose one of the kids, usually the most curious, and ask him to look very closely.

After he is quite certain and has convinced me beyond any doubt that there is no hole, I ask him to close his eyes and concentrate. I then proceed with the trick. More often than not, the kids let out a gasp and then everyone wants to have a look.

Stuck On You
Static balloons

First, you're showing the children the fun and amazing magic of static electricity and the next thing you know, you're out buying those laundry products that make sure the fun and amazing magic leaves your socks alone.

Props: One balloon.

The Old How-To:

(1) Blow up one balloon. (2) On a wool sweater, a flannel shirt, a piece of cloth or your hair, rub the balloon several times *in one direction*. (3) Place on shirt, the wall or the ceiling and it will cling.

The Old Razzle-Dazzle:

This is one of those things that seems to be more fun when the kids are doing it themselves. Once they have learned how to do it they'll have great fun inventing uses and games of their own.

However, not to be left out of the fun, blow up a balloon and knot it.

Rub it as explained. Hold it out in front of you in your left hand. Slowly place it behind your back allowing it to cling to the back of your shirt. I do this with exaggerated movements and sometimes announce I have just discovered how to make a balloon disappear.

Bring your hand in front of you again. Notice that your hand is empty. Look very closely at your hand.

Slowly look up to see if it might be floating above you then down to the floor to see if it may have fallen.

Finally, turn around so your back is to the children. They will call out that it is on your back. Pretend not to hear. Play this up a while. The kids will have a great time calling out directions to you which you can't seem to get right.

To finish you discover the balloon on your back or it may fall off during this silly show. Anyway, hold the balloon in both hands. Look embarassed. Then with one of your hands squeeze the balloon so that it pops, startling you, the children and giving everyone a good laugh.

Hokum-Pokum

Simple Magical Stunts

It's amazing what you can do
with "Nothing in my hands
and nothing up my sleeve".

Look, No Hands
The floating cup

This little beaut is a real shocker. Perfectly suited for picnics, hot dog stands, donut shops and the like, it can be done spontaneously just about anywhere with the same eerie result.

Props: One Styrofoam coffee cup.

The Old How-To:

(1) Stand up and position yourself slightly away from your audience. This will protect the sight angles. (2) After drinking the contents of the cup, poke your right thumb through the side that's closest to you. You might want to "cough" to cover the sound. (3) Rest the cup on your left palm and, with everyone watching, move your right fingers away from the cup, leaving your thumb in the hole. (4) Now *slowly* move your left hand away and the cup will appear to be floating. After it "floats" for a while, grip it again and appear to finish your drink.

The Old Razzle-Dazzle:

It's best to be subtle in order to achieve the full effect of this stunt. Be casual as you sip your coffee or tea. When you have finished, slip your thumb into the side of the cup but continue "drinking" as if there is nothing the matter.

Now move to a position where there is no one behind you and you are standing apart from everyone else. Partly talking to yourself but doing it loud enough to be heard, utter something like, "Hmmm, I wonder if I can still do this. It used to be so easy." Make your moves slowly. Most people will think you are going to attempt some balancing feat.

"Would everyone please be still? I have to concentrate. This can be a little tricky sometimes." Slowly move your fingers away. Pause.

Take a deep breath and very slowly move your left hand away. It should appear as if you are balancing the cup in the air. The gasps of surprise are wonderful.

Once I was doing this at a family gathering at my aunt's house. She was concerned she wouldn't be able to get the coffee stains out of her new carpet if the cup were to fall.

This same principle is adaptable to almost anything you can put your thumb into. You might try apples, oranges, muffins, dinner rolls or donuts. All can magically become lighter than air!

Here's Looking at You

How to see through a blindfold

As a kid, I was convinced my parents had eyes in the back of their heads and could even see through walls. As a parent, I can definitely see an advantage to being suspected of such talents.

Props:

One piece of dark cloth about 4 inches wide and long enough to tie around your head.

The Old How-To:

(1) Lay the cloth flat in front of you and fold one of the hems to the center of the cloth.

(2) Fold the opposite hem to the center as well, slightly overlapping the first hem.

(3) Hold the cloth in both hands, fingers beneath, thumbs on top.

(4) Hold the cloth up to cover your eyes with the seams toward your eyes but separate the hems a bit with your thumbs. You will be able to see through the single thickness of cloth.

(5) Prepare to mystify.

The Old Razzle-Dazzle:

The possibilities of this great little prop are limitless. After I have folded the blindfold, I cover one of the children's eyes, *making certain that the hems of the cloth are still overlapping.* This will help prove the cloth is legit.

Then I have the kids tie the blindfold on me as I hold it in place. Of course I deftly separate the hems of the cloth, but I pretend not to be able to see at all. I start feeling my way around the room and suddenly we are in the middle of a squealing game of "catch me if you can."

The children have a very difficult time containing their laughter as you grope around trying to catch them. I can still remember the thrill when a grown-up is "it."

You can have them hide objects in the room and you find them with uncanny ease. The kids will go out of their way to stump you, but remember: The Great Dadd-O sees all, knows all and is the champion of "pin the tail."

Where Did It Go?

A pencil vanishes into thin hair

I don't think he was really a relative but we all called him Uncle George. We loved it when he came around because it always meant pockets full of candy and a few unexpected tricks up his sleeves. This one was so characteristic of Uncle George's repertoire.

Props: One pencil and one coin, a quarter is fine.

The Old How-To:

(1) Hold quarter on your flat right palm. (2) Raise the pencil in the left hand as if going to strike the coin. (3) As your hand comes alongside your left ear, leave the pencil behind your ear and continue with a downward motion, striking the coin with your fingers. The pencil has vanished (of course this is silly! Read the Razzle-Dazzle).

The Old Razzle-Dazzle:

Uncle George, a bumbler at best, always fancied himself a magician. Try as he may, things always seemed to go wrong for him to the delight of his young little audience.

First, he would reach into his pocket and fish out a quarter. He would carefully shine it on his sleeve then lay it on his outstretched hand.

Next, he would bring out his magic pencil. It looked like any ordinary pencil to us but he would reassure us that it was special. "Why, with just a little tap of this pencil I can make things disappear. Watch."

He would raise the pencil and bring it down on the coin. The kids would all start snickering when the coin was still there. Uncle George looked genuinely confused. He'd try again and again the coin remained.

"Maybe something is wrong with the batteries." He's give the pencil a good shake in the air and then a few good taps on his head.

Stifling our giggles we would patiently wait for poor Uncle George to try it once again.

Slowly he would raise the pencil. He paused then swiftly struck the coin. It took us a minute to realize that something had backfired again. "Darn, where did it go to now?" Uncle George's pencil, his magic pencil had vanished without a trace.

He scratched his head and slowly turned his head as if looking to see where the pencil had gotten to. Once he had done this we would all see the pencil behind his ear. Of course when we tried to tell him where it was he would pretend to misunderstand and reach for the wrong ear, milking the silliness of the moment.

Letters From . . .
How to write magic messages to your children

When we were youngsters, my brother and I would spend many an eerie hour scaring ourselves with our ouija board. This little bluff eliminates the board but not the mystery and fun.

Props:
Two small squares of paper and one pencil with eraser and sharp point.

The Old How-To:

(1) Before demonstrating your "skill", write a brief message on a small piece of paper in another room and roll it into a small ball. Hold this secretly in your right hand.

(2) When you're ready to perform, present the child with a sharply pointed pencil and a piece of blank paper. Have him roll his paper into a ball and give it to you.

(3) Ask the child to place the pencil on the table with the eraser down and point in the air. While this attention is focused on putting the pencil into the proper position, switch the two paper balls, placing the one with your message on the tip of the pencil.

The Old Razzle-Dazzle:

The more mysterious the better. You might try doing this by candlelight or wait for a good old-fashioned thunderstorm.

"Do you believe in ghosts?" Pause. "Well, I didn't for the longest time until one day I got a note from a spook named Fred." Wait for the kids' reaction.

"I'm telling you I really do have a ghost friend and his name really is Fred. You don't believe me? I suppose you want me to prove it to you." But of course!

Have one of the children roll the paper into a ball. This lets you show there is nothing on the paper and that there are no tricks, right?

Have one of the other children position the pencil, point up, on the table. Take the paper ball from your assistant and put it into the hand that you have the message ball hidden in. You can then switch the balls as you are handing the pencil to your second assistant.

Continued . . .

46

Now comes the time to call on the spirits. You can play it spooky to get the kids on the edge of their seats.

"Hey, Fred, I have some people here who don't think you are real. Do you have anything you want to say to them?" Wait a minute for Fred to write his note.

Remove the message ball from the pencil point and read it aloud. If one of the kids is having a birthday, it might be fun to write a spirit message along those lines.

One evening, Eve and I were having some milk and cookies when Eve suddenly got up, grabbed a cookie and ran out of the room. She returned a short time later but without the cookie.

Before I could ask she said, "Fred wanted a cookie."

Lost and Found

A simple yet effective card trick

Every father should know at least one card trick. It comes in handy many times over and this simple dodge and its variations can make you look like a wizard of the "pasteboards".

Props: One deck of cards.

The Old How-To:

(1) Have someone select a card, and look at it. While they are looking at their card, note the card on the bottom of the deck. *This is the key card.* (2) Square the deck and place it on the table. Have the selected card placed on top of the deck. Now the "mystery" card is on top and you know which card is on the bottom of the deck. Your goal is to get them next to each other in the pile. (3) Have someone cut the deck. Now it's in two piles. When you replace the bottom half on the top half, your card will be on top of the mystery card. They can now cut again and again. (4) Turn the cards over one at a time until you come to your card. The next one will be the mystery card.

The Old Razzle-Dazzle:

As I said, there are several variations on this effect and if you carefully guard the secret of the key card you can astound your audience many times over without them catching on to you.

My favorite way to reveal the chosen card is set up as if you have made a mistake. First of all, have the card selected and returned to the deck as described.

Turn the cards to face you and shuffle through them as if trying to decide which card it could be. Look puzzled and shuffle through some more. Actually you are looking for the key card. Once you locate it remember the card that is directly in front of it.

"You know this is my best trick. I don't know too many but this one I do very well. Ah, hah!" Take a card, any card and show it to the one who chose. "Here is your card!" This will raise a few chuckles as everyone loves it when a magician muffs it, be sure it is the wrong card.

Continued . . .

"Oh, wait, don't tell me! I think I've got it now!" Again it's the wrong card. Act real confused. "I've never had trouble with it before! Let me try one more time."

Start dealing the cards out face up. Become noticeably frantic. Deal them faster. When you come to the chosen card keep dealing. This will totally convince them that you have really messed things up.

Stop, holding a card in your hand about to deal it out. "Now the next card I turn over has got to be your card." The kids will let you know you are wrong. "No, now I know the next card is the one you've chosen. In fact, I am so sure that the next card I turn over will be the card that I'll bet you."

Seldom can a kid pass up such a sure thing. Let them make their wager then nonchalantly fish through the cards and turn the right card face down. It is a delicious moment when they realize they have been had.

A second variation has an air of mystery about it as it is all done silently. Have the card selected and cut into the deck as described.

Without saying a word, turn the deck over and spread the cards out on the table.

Hold your hand a few inches above the cards and move it over the cards as if trying to pick up the vibrations. Here you will note the key card and the chosen card on top of it.

Dramatically reach out with your other hand and lightly touch your assistant's forehead a la mindreader. Pause a moment, smile faintly and remove the chosen card, laying it in front of the mystified youngster.

Now that you know the principal behind this little wonder play around with ways of your own to reveal the selected card. With a little imagination there is no telling where it may turn up.

What's Holding Things Up?

How to make a pencil appear suspended

This is one of those oldies-but-goodies that has fallen by the wayside and only needs to be dusted off a little to be a shining gem.

Props: One pencil or pen.

The Old How-To:

(1) Lay the pencil across your left palm and grip your wrist as shown in the photo. (2) As you flip your hand over so the back is facing your audience — a movement you make with great exaggeration — slide your *right* index finger over the pencil, pinning it to your palm. It will appear suspended behind your hand. (3) When you think your audience is beginning to "figure you out," suddenly use your *left* thumb to hold the pencil and take your right hand away. Since they will have started to suspect the right hand, this should throw them off guard again.

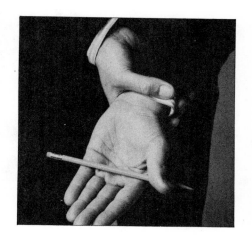

The Old Razzle-Dazzle:

"I know I am an attractive person. I know this because things are always sticking to me. I'm like a magnet. No, really. Take this pencil, for example." Pick up the pencil and put it on the palm of your hand.

"Watch how it just clings to me." Turn your hand over, allowing the pencil to fall to the floor. "That's odd. It must be the humidity or something like that." Repeat the same action.

"I don't understand it. Maybe I'm losing my charge." With this, rub your palm briskly on your trouser leg as if charging it with static electricity.

With your hand charged and ready to go, follow through with the routine by holding the pencil in place with your right index finger.

Pause for a moment to allow the illusion to sink in. "There, you see? Just like I told you." Turn your back to the front, reversing your moves so that you return to just having the pencil laying across your palm.

For an encore, set it up the same way but this time pin the pencil with your left thumb rather than your right finger. Then say: "This has always puzzled me." Remove your right hand hold and scratch your head. Turn your back front again, reversing the moves. "I don't know if I will ever figure it out. I guess I'll just have to get used to being so attractive."

Getting The Lead Out
The vanishing pencil

This is a little diversion that can come in handy to break the tedium of a bout of homework.

Props: One pencil and one sheet of notebook paper.

The Old How-To:

(1) Lay the paper flat on a table, place the pencil on the paper and then roll the pencil up in the paper. (2) With one end of the tube slightly below the edge of the table, twist the other end of the paper tube shut. While twisting that end, ease your grip on the pencil, allowing it to slide out and into your lap. (Don't let it fall on the floor because it might make a clatter.) (3) Turn the tube over and twist the other end shut, being careful not to crush the shape of the tube. (4) Hold the tube upright in the center of the table and smash down the tube with your hand, allowing the pencil to fall off your lap at the same time. It will seem as if the pencil passed through the table top.

The Old Razzle-Dazzle:

Begin by taking the pencil and holding it end up near the center of the table. Bring the other hand down on the pencil as if trying to smash in through the table. Pretend to hurt your hand slightly.

"I must be getting soft. I used to be able to do this with no trouble." Take a sheet of paper and roll up the pencil in it.

Once you have twisted the ends shut, again hold the tube end up toward the center of the table. Pretend to test the cushion of the paper with the palm of your hand. "There, that's better. Let's see if I can still do this." Hold your striking hand high.

On the count of three, smash your hand down on the paper tube, allowing the pencil to fall from your lap. "Yep, haven't lost my touch."

A Real Cut-up

How to slice a banana without taking off the skin

This stunt could very well rank you with Zorro, Captain Blood, the Scarlet Pimpernel or at least one of the Three Musketeers. The kids think I'm crazy whenever I start this trick. But when they peel the banana, their eyes pop out of their heads!

INVISIBLE SWORD

Props: One golden ripe banana, one needle and some heavy thread.

The Old How-To:

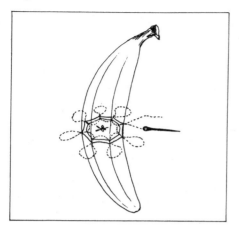

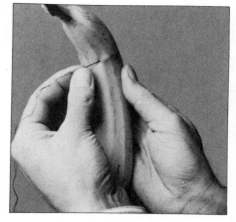

You will be circling the *inside* of the banana with a piece of thread.

(1) Insert the needle into one of the banana's ridges about 1-1/2 inches from the tip. Guide the needle along the *inside* of the banana to the next ridge, pulling the needle out at that point.

(2) Return the needle into the *same hole,* leaving slack in the thread as you guide the needle to the next ridge. Repeat this action until the thread has gone completely around the banana and

the needle is pulled out the *same hole* you began with.

(3) Now take the *two ends* of the thread and pull the thread out of the hole. The thread will cut through the meat of the banana without damaging the skin.

(4) Repeat this at 1-1/2 to 2-inch intervals, cutting the banana into three to four parts. Note: Prepare the banana no more than 3 hours prior to the stunt or it will start to turn black.

The Old Razzle-Dazzle:

"When I was a child, I used to love watching the old swashbuckler films, and afterward I would spend hours having sword fights with invisible enemies sent in by the wicked king.

"Some of my friends made swords out of wood, but I never had one. I found that I could become an excellent swordsman just by using my imagination — good enough to take on Errol Flynn himself!"

Continued . . .

Here I bring out the prepared banana. "Let me demonstrate."

I give the banana to one of the kids and have him hold it out in front of him in one hand. Then I pretend to draw my sword and take a few practice swipes in the air.

I adjust the child's hold so that the banana is being held out horizontally by the stem. Dramatically, I swing my "sword" down toward the banana. "That's one," Again. "That's two." And once more. "That's three."

I put my sword away and begin to bow. I then look around slightly confused. "Oh, I see, you didn't see." I take back the banana and begin to peel it. As the pieces fall out I say, "That's one and that's two and that's three."

Then with my hand on my trusty sword, I wave my hand in the air as I take a deep, courtly bow.

———————————

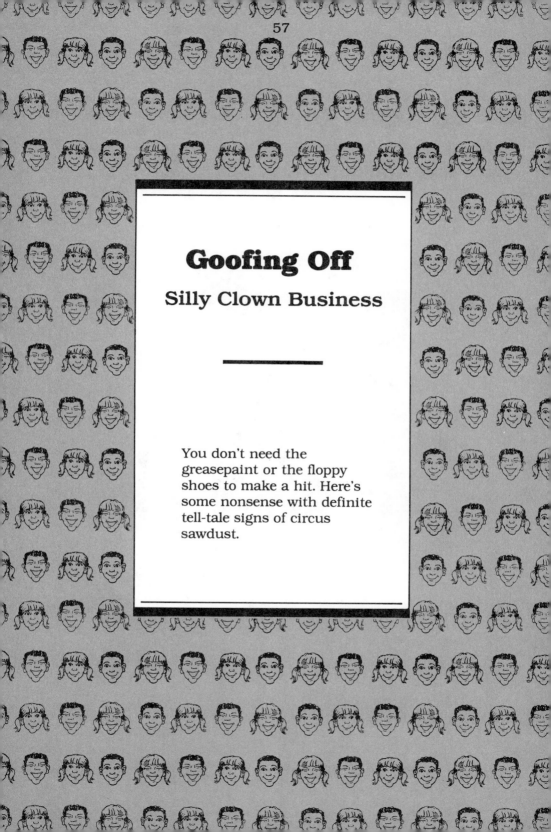

Goofing Off

Silly Clown Business

You don't need the greasepaint or the floppy shoes to make a hit. Here's some nonsense with definite tell-tale signs of circus sawdust.

Not A Leg To Stand On

How to make your leg disappear

Being equally absurd, this goofy stunt is the perfect match for the "appearing shoe." It's a fine element of clowning when something appears obvious — except to the fool who is trying to do the fooling.

Props: One large piece of cloth or a small towel big enough to hide your legs from the knees down.

The Old How-To:

(1) Hold the cloth by its corners so it just touches the floor and hides your legs below your knees. Shake the cloth slightly for effect. (Again, if you are wearing shoes with laces, loosen them before you begin.) (2) Slip one foot out of the loosened shoe and bend your leg back at the knee while you balance on the other leg. (3) Raise the cloth slowly towards your waist, stopping just before the hem reaches the knee. It will appear as if your leg has vanished. (4) Lower the cloth to its original position and replace your foot into your show. Pull the cloth away with a flourish as you bow.

The Old Razzle-Dazzle:

Be dramatic and flamboyant while performing this act of nonsense. I use a kazoo during the act to lend all the more to the madness.

I begin the routine by taking a bow and unfolding the cloth with a snap. Next, I cover my legs.

I raise the cloth with my leg still in place, then lower it. I do this again. The third time, I get out of the shoe and bend my leg back.

The kids will often heckle me, but it's all in fun. Moving right along, I repeat the trick with my other leg.

And here's another chapter in the case of the missing feet. I stand in front of a sturdy table and do the same build-up, only this time both legs disappear at the same time. Of course, the trick is that I'm actually sitting on the edge of the table.

If this is done quickly, it can catch the kids off guard and be a real shocker for them. Of course, what goes up must come down. Lower your legs and take a brief pause before whipping away the cloth and taking an exaggerated bow.

Blow, Gabriel, Blow!

The old Bronx cheer

My older brother was sent home from school one day for doing this during a class discussion. The principal, teacher and my parents were not very pleased. I thought he was a genius.

Props: The nipple of a balloon and one handkerchief or tissue.

The Old How-To:

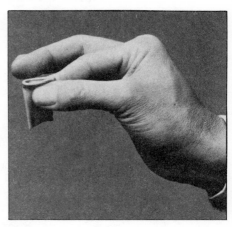

(1) Hold the balloon piece between your thumb and first finger. Practice, practice, practice blowing into it until you can make a rasping noise. When you perfect this . . . (2) Fake a sneeze. Just as you're finishing your "ah, ah, ah . . . " (and just before the "choo!"), put the handkerchief to your nose and, under cover of the hankie, put the balloon piece to your lips and blow. It should make a delightfully rude sound.

The Old Razzle-Dazzle:

And now for a bit of burlesque. Let's admit it: Every kid — and every adult, for that matter — is a natural-born comic when it comes to sneezing, belching or farting. So in tribute to the whoopee cushion, plastic puke and the Three Stooges, I offer this cute touch of crass.

You can carry this with you wherever you go and always be ready for some riotous fun. The build-up can get some laughs, but the payoff comes when you grab your hankie and let go. When you are done, fold up the hankie with the balloon piece inside and put it in your pocket as you excuse yourself.

For those who opt against the handkerchief, you can get the same effect by going in for the sneeze with both hands, the right covering the left. Pause a moment after the blow before lowering your hands and making a comment like, "Oh, no, I forgot my handkerchief!"

Then you can wipe your hands on your shirt or trousers — or, better yet, on someone else's shirt. It's amazing how the kids love this innocent little "gross out."

The Big Squeeze
Squirting a fake bottle of ketchup

When I was a kid, I used to delight in terrorizing my cousins with this trick bottle at family picnics. It wasn't until my brother grabbed the wrong bottle and actually squirted ketchup all over cousin Nancy that I realized the brilliance of this invention.

Props:

One squeeze bottle, the kind used for ketchup or mustard; about one foot of string (red string would be great).

The Old How-To:

(1.) Cut off just enough of the bottle's tip so the string can move freely through the opening, then thread the string through the tip. (2.) Knot both ends of the string with knots large enough that they won't go through the opening. (3.) Feed the string into the bottle and screw on the top. When you squeeze the bottle, the string will squirt out just like the real thing.

The Old Razzle-Dazzle:

At the family picnic, as the hot dogs and burgers are coming off the grill and everyone is busy dressing up their little feast, slyly bring out the fake bottle of ketchup.

Pretend to squeeze ketchup onto your burger. Look puzzled when nothing comes out of the bottle. Try again with the same result.

"Maybe it's empty." Shake the bottle. "No, there's plenty in it."

Try unsuccessfully to squeeze out some more. "Maybe it's stuck." Look into the tip. "No, I don't see anything. Do you?" Turn to your unsuspecting victim.

Wait until he has come in close enough, then give the bottle a good squeeze. He will jump back with horror and think the worst while you, everyone around and eventually the victim all have a good laugh.

It might then be wise to move, just in case your stooge is into revenge.

Father's Nose is Best
How to balance a balloon on your nose

Imagine you're at little Nicki's birthday party and Slappy Happy the Clown is late in arriving. The little natives are getting restless. Suddenly, in a flash of inspiration, you and your clever nose step into the spotlight.

Props: One small round balloon and rubber cement.

The Old How-To:

(1) Blow up the balloon but don't tie it. Place a dab of rubber cement on it. Let the cement dry, then let the air out of the balloon.

(2) Apply a thin but generous coat of cement to your nose and let it dry. Experiment with the amount and placement of glue for maximum hold.

The Old Razzle-Dazzle:

The success of this trick is in the old sucker build-up; the third time's the charm.

Begin with balloon deflated. "Ladies and gentlemen . . . You are about to witness an incredible feat of skill and daring never before attempted by a rational, clear-thinking individual." With this ballyhoo, blow up and knot the balloon.

"And now I, the Great Daddo, will balance this balloon on this nose, and I will do it while standing on one foot." Pause. "I must ask for complete silence please." This last request, of course, will invite the opposite.

Now stand with your head tilted back. With the utmost concentration, place the balloon on your nose, making certain not to connect the glue spots. Hold your hands away and let the balloon fall.

Again, go through the motions with the same result. "This is not as easy as it looks," you explain. "Please bear with me once more."

This time, connect the glue spots. Slowly take your hands away. Move from side to side as if you're trying to maintain balance.

While the kids are applauding, lower your head. The balloon will remain stuck in place and the kids will come unglued.

As you exit, pull at the balloon as if it is permanently stuck to your face. And, suddenly, a star is born.

Sticking It Out

Pretending your tongue is attached to your Adam's apple

This silliness is great to use on a grumpy child when all else has failed. Keep doing it and keep smiling; the frown can't help but blossom into a smile, and nothing is more heart-warming to a parent.

Props: Just yourself.

The Old How-To:

(1) As you push in your Adam's apple with your right index finger, stick out your tongue. (2) Leave your tongue out and take the finger away from your Adam's apple. (3) As you pull your right ear lobe with your right hand, retract your tongue. (4) Repeat, repeat, repeat.

The Old Razzle-Dazzle:

Begin very slowly so the child has time to understand the pattern you're creating. Take your time, then progressively go faster and faster. You can add your own variations such as crossing your eyes as you touch your nose.

You might beep the child's nose or push his Adam's apple. Sometimes the child will pick up on the game and create his own responses. If he stubbornly refuses to lighten up say, "Gee, yours seems to be broken. I guess we'll have to call a repairman to fix it."

After you have set up the pattern, let him push your Adam's apple or beep your nose. For some reason this really tickles the kids and they seem to remember it a long time, so you have to remember as well. Keep all this silliness in the back of your mind so when you get a sudden poke in the Adam's apple you'll know how to respond. There's nothing worse than a dad who seems to be out of order.

How Does Your Garden Grow?

The wilting flower

I first saw this bit of whimsy performed by a clown in a circus. In all its simplicity, it has never failed to charm a smile or two. I often find this a nice way to mend hurt feelings or to break the ice with a particularly shy child.

Props: One long-stemmed flower (real or artificial)

The Old How-To:

(1) Hold the flower vertically, grasping it at the base of the stem between the thumb and first finger. (2) By easing the pressure slightly, you will note that the weight of the bud will cause the stem to pivot between your fingers, allowing the flower to fall over. (3) Experiment with the pressure to control the "rate of wilt."

The Old Razzle-Dazzle:

The success of this routine lies in its simplicity.

Begin by smelling the flower and react — or rather over-react — to its fragrance. You might pantomime delight or you might go for the laugh and fake a sneeze. If you choose to sneeze, a slow wilt of the flower will secure a chuckle.

After you have enjoyed the flower's smell, make your approach to a child, offering to let her smell the flower, too.

Be deliberate; be coy; be shy. Perhaps you might mimic the shy child's gestures. Once you are close enough for the child to smell the flower, hold it out to her, and as she moves to take a whiff, let the flower wilt.

Pull back in surprise and set the flower upright again. Move in again and let the flower wilt once more. Move on to another child and let her smell the flower. No wilt. Another; no wilt again.

Go back to the first child. Again, as she moves in to smell the flower, let it wilt. This action will really get the kids giggling.

For a finish, move in one more time and let the child smell and keep the flower.

If you have another flower, I have a follow-up that could keep your little audience laughing a little longer.

The Short End
Of The Stem
This Bud's
Not for You

The same clown I once saw do the "Wilting Flower" would continue the merriment with this inspired little twist. The surprise of it made everyone laugh outright.

Props: Yet another long-stemmed flower.

The Old How-To:

(1) Cut the flower's stem about 1½ inches from the bud. Hold the flower between thumb and index finger right at the cut so your fingers are actually holding the flower together. (2) When you present the flower to a child, hold it slightly higher than normal. That way, she will grab the bottom of the stem below the cut. (3) As the child takes hold of the stem, you walk away with the flower portion.

The Old Razzle-Dazzle:

Though this can stand on its own as a quick gag, it truly shines as a sequel to the "Wilting Flower."

After you have done your turn with the wilted flower, take up another flower. Again you smell it; again you sneeze.

Now start to hand it to a pretty little girl. Just as she reaches for it, change your mind and start to hand it to someone else.

Again, change your mind. You can actually get the kids cheering as you try to decide who you'll finally give it to.

Make your choice at last. Approach the child slowly, building up to the surprise. As she takes the stem, walk away holding the flower. Of course, after the laugh you will want to give the flower to her for keeps.

If you don't have several children to play off each other, one will do. You may not get belly-laughs but smiles are guaranteed.

That's Shoe Biz!

Making a magical hump appear to grow under a cloth

Your audience will be expecting something totally different than what actually happens here. The surprising absurdity makes this bit a good spontaneous bid for a laugh. Admittedly, this is a real dumb trick. Be ready to play it like Johnny Carson does when a joke falls flat.

Props: One large piece of cloth. A large dinner napkin or towel will do.

The Old How-To:

(1) Hold a cloth with the corners stretched between your hands. Bend over and lower the cloth so its bottom hem just touches the floor directly in front of your right foot. If you are wearing shoes that tie, loosen the laces of your right shoe before you begin.

(2) Under this cover, slip your foot out of the shoe with as little movement as possible.

(3) Slowly lower the cloth down over shoe to cover it entirely. Then whisk away the cloth to reveal the miraculous appearance.

The Old Razzle-Dazzle:

To ensure the element of surprise, begin by telling a mysterious tale.

"In India, there are magicians who do incredible things in the streets and marketplaces. They are known as fakirs. Some people call them fakes for short.

"There are many stories of these magicians suspending ropes in thin air, walking on coals and flying on magic carpets. They say that some of these fakirs actually grow trees from little sprouts in a matter of minutes.

"First, they would pick a place where the ground was right for growing and then they would plant their little sprouts." Pretend to plant the sprouts. "Second, they would cover the spot with a magic cloth much like this one." Shake out the cloth, spread it on the floor in front of you and step back.

"Then they would wait." Fold your arms and wait for a minute, then look puzzled. "That's odd, it shouldn't take any time at all. Maybe if we all chant the word Alakahlakammako, it will speed things up."

Continued . . .

Get everyone chanting any silly word. Lift the cloth by the corners nearest you as if you are checking on things, but you are actually screening your right foot.

Give the cloth slight shakes to cover the motion of you removing your foot from the shoe. Now lower the cloth down over the shoe, giving it slight shakes as you go. It will appear as if something actually is growing under the cloth.

When the shoe is completely covered, step back. No one will notice your stocking foot. "Well, look at that!" Move in and whisk the cloth away.

"Here we have a . . . What's that?" Look amazed; the kids will be just as amazed as you for a moment before they realize what has happened and their amazement becomes amusement.

Look equally as surprised when you "realize" that it is your shoe.

———————

Hand-Jive

Tricks with Hands

―――――

No matter what they say
about idle hands there is a
wealth of fun in four fingers
and a thumb.

The Mysterious Daddy's Finger

How to carry your "spare finger" in a box

This trick held an eerie fascination for me when I was a child. My brother would add to the effect by chilling his finger on a piece of ice before showing it to me. It's a perfect follow-up to the "Detachable Digit" or will stand very well on its own.

Props:
A small cardboard jewelry box (like the kind cuff links come in) and some cotton.

The Old How-To:

(1.) Cut a hole *near one end* of the bottom of the box. The hole should be large enough for your ring finger to fit to the second joint. (2.) Insert the finger through the hole and push it through the cotton. Your finger should look as if it is laying in the box and being cushioned by the cotton.

The Old Razzle-Dazzle:

I begin by telling a little-known "fact" before removing the box from my pocket.

"I used to have this terrible problem of my fingers falling off when I least expected it. One day, one fell off into my soup. It was very embarrassing. Finally, one fell off while I was washing my hands and it went down the drain. Now I always carry a spare." Then I remove the box from my pocket and place it on the palm of my left hand.

"Would you like to see it?" Need I ask?

Now slowly, very slowly, I remove the lid to the box. This gives me the perfect cover to slip my finger into the box. With the finger in place, I hold the open box for everyone to see. "It looks very real, doesn't it? It even feels real." I say, "Go on, touch it if you want to." Be sure to have the finger completely relaxed to enhance the effect.

This makes a very strong impression on impressionable minds. My brother had me and my friends going on this one for quite a long time until we sneaked a peek in the box when he wasn't around. Even then, I thought he had just lost another finger.

Make your getaway by merely replacing the lid, putting the box into your left pocket and removing your finger there.

Just Poking Around

The clever art of sticking your finger in your ear.

This is another in the long line of classic nonsense that never fails to win a smile or two from the little ones. My little Eve is convinced that poor dad's noodle is quite empty, and she is always looking in one ear to find out if she can see light from the other side.

Props: One ear, one finger

The Old How-To:

(1) Place the tip of your right index finger in your right ear. Pretend to push the finger into the ear, actually curling the finger back to the middle knuckle.

(2) Simultaneously press out your left cheek with the tip of your tongue. It should look as if you have poked your finger clear through to your opposite cheek.

(3) Keeping the knuckle in place, move your hand up and down as if scratching. Move your tongue up and down, matching the movement of your finger. Don't forget to relax your tongue as you "remove" your finger from your ear.

The Old Razzle-Dazzle:

You can perform this whenever you'd like, but I have always had great success with it when a child asks me a question. Since I already have his attention, I can get right to the trick.

After he has asked his question, I pause, tapping my index finger on my chin.

Pretending to really concentrate on an answer, I move my tapping finger to my temple. "Hmmm, this is going to take some thinking, I think."

Then I scratch my head as I keep a look of deep concentration on my face. "This is going to take some real brain scratching, I'm afraid." With this, I place my finger in my ear, moving it up and down as my tongue moves down and up on the other side of my face.

Making the appropriate hems and haws, I finally remove my finger from my ear, point skyward and declare, "Eureka!" Then the answer to the question — if it's not already forgotten — is given.

Bending Over Backwards
Making your fingers look double-jointed

The kids might think it's a bit odd when you appear at the dinner table wearing a pair of oversized mittens. But then, the more you amaze them with little stunts from this book, the more they'll come to accept the fact that Pop is a bit off the wall.

Props: One pair of oversized mittens or gardening gloves.

The Old How-To:

(1) On your left hand, put one glove on backwards, leaving the thumb empty. (Note: You might want to stuff some paper into the empty thumb to give it some substance.) On the other hand, put on the glove properly. (2) Place both hands on the table with the palms of both *gloves* downward. (Since one glove is on backwards, the palm of that *hand* will really be facing up, but both hands will appear to be resting normally on the table.) (3) By bending the fingers of your left hand, it will appear that you are double-jointed. (Note: You may want to wear long sleeves to hide your wrists.)

The Old Razzle-Dazzle:

This is a particularly good stunt to use while rough-housing with the boys. Tell them you're going to show them a few boxing moves, which gives you a great excuse for wearing the gloves.

You can either choose a sparing partner or do some shadow-boxing. Either way, you have to fake a punch. You might smash the wall or, for comedy's sake, punch yourself on the jaw.

Now the fun begins. Grab your hand as if you have hurt it, but keep this part of the action light so you don't upset the kids. Say something like, "Boy, that was dumb. I think it's okay, though. It does hurt a little. I'd better check it just to make sure."

Put your hands on the table. With your right hand, bend one of the left hand fingers back. "Well, look at that!" Bend back another finger and another.

Pause and say, "That's funny, I could never do that before."

Play with it a while longer and then say, "I don't think it's broken but I'd better check to make sure." With this, remove the glove from the left hand. Examine the hand closely and give it a shake. Now try to bend the fingers back, but to no avail. "That's funny. I must have just knocked the joints loose for a minute." Shrug and continue wrestling as if nothing happened.

The Daring Detachable Digit
How to take off your thumb

This little stunt has been around forever and has grown to become a true classic. It has been performed countless times to the delight and awe of youngsters and has kept many a father, uncle and older brother in constant demand. This could very well become your "reputation maker."

Props: You will need your two thumbs.

The Old How-To:

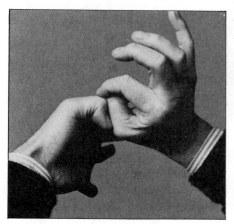 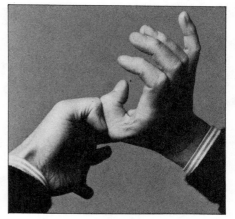

(1) Place your hands as shown in the first photo. This view shows how *you* will be viewing *your* thumbs. Both thumbs are bent at 90-degree angles. The only hard part is getting into this position. Practice! (2) Keeping your thumbs in this position, move your index finger over to cover the "gap" between your thumbs (see second photo). To the audience, this will make it look like you have one continuous thumb. (3) As you move your hands apart slightly, it will appear as if your thumb is broken in two because the index finger still hides the "gap." (4) This entire trick is based on proper "line of sight." If your audience sees your bent thumbs, the jig is up. Show this trick to one person at a time so the sight angle is perfect. Practice while looking in the mirror until it looks right.

The Old Razzle-Dazzle:

Begin this trick with a build-up. I start by wearing a bandage on my right thumb. Since attention is drawn to my thumb, I explain: "You know, it's the darnedest thing, but my thumb keeps falling off. I've been afraid of losing it so I've been wearing this Band-aid. You don't believe me do you? Well, here, I'll show you." With this, I remove the bandage. Then I give my thumb a slight shake. "That's funny, it usually just drops off." Another shake and a tug. "Maybe it's stuck."

This bit of business can be played until you have the kids really going. Finally, pause and compare thumbs. "Ah, there's the trouble. It was the wrong thumb." Proceed with the routine.

You might also try making a whistling sound as you slide the tip. It will help focus attention on the action. Use your imagination and have fun. Don't forget to finish by putting the bandage back on your left thumb.

Give That Man a Hand

Making it look like you're inflating your hand

And yet another in the parade of classic sight gags and silly bits of business. This one has a certain charm for my daughter, who is always trying to let the air out of my hand.

Props: Your hand.

The Old How-To:

(1) Bend your fingers to the palm of your right hand as if you're making a fist, but stick out your right thumb. (2) Pretend to blow into your thumb like you're blowing up a balloon. (3) As you blow, slowly unfold your hand until the fingers are fully extended. It should appear that your hand is filling with air.

The Old Razzle-Dazzle:

This is a great gag to pull when you are meeting a child for the first time.

First, hold out your hand to shake someone's hand. If it's a boy, pretend that his grip was too tight and come away holding your hand as if it hurts.

Hold your hand in a fist like it's cramped and shake it slightly. Sometimes the kids are really worried that they may have hurt you, so reassure them that you are all right. "Oh, don't worry about it. I can fix it in no time."

Take a deep breath and blow into your thumb. Make it appear to be a bit of an effort before you actually start unfolding your fingers.

Stop blowing as your hand reaches its normal state. You may want to make a hissing sound with your mouth as if the air is leaking out of your thumb. Pretend to tie a knot at the tip of your thumb.

Wiggle your fingers around a little to make sure they are working properly. "There, good as new."

With a smile, offer your hand again to show there was no harm done.

The Retractable Reach

How to make your arm appear to shrink

This is another stunt my brother fooled me with many years ago. I went around thinking I could actually shrink my arm. After trying to convince me otherwise, my mother finally conceded it was natural for everyone to shrink their arms and that I was not strange. The charm of this stunt is that after you have demonstrated your skill, the kids will have a go at it and the gag will become even more of a mystery.

Props: One or several impressionable children

The Old How-To:

(1) Start with both arms extended, as shown. Call your audience's attention to the fact that both arms are the same length. (2) While one arm remains stationary, rotate the other 360 degrees, starting in a downward motion and bringing it up behind you, over your head and finishing back where you started, *keeping it* *extended the entire time.* (3) Your body will naturally shift during this process. When your arm returns to its original position, it will unaccountably be two or three inches shorter than the stationary arm. (Don't ask *me* why — I'm a clown, not a scientist!)

The Old Razzle-Dazzle:

The trick works by itself and can be as mysterious as it is entertaining. I usually start by saying to the kids: "Did you know I can make my left arm shorter than my right arm? In fact, everyone can. They just don't seem to know they can. I didn't think it was true, either, until I tried it one day."

It's always good to begin with some ridiculous claim of this sort. It challenges the curiosity.

"It's really all in the way you look at things. If you look at them one way, you may never see that they could be another way." Suiting action to words, proceed with the demonstration.

This would make a good companion for the "Long Arm of the Pa."

The Long Arm of the Pa
How to stretch your arm

This little stunt comes in very handy in making it a game to pick up toys after a hard day of play. It's also a good follow-up to the Retractable Reach.

Props: No props are required. Just wear a shirt or jacket with long, loose sleeves.

The Old How-To:

(1) Stand with your right side to the audience, your left arm extended in front of you. (2) The effect is achieved by simply moving your left shoulder forward while your right hand makes a pulling motion on your left wrist. It should look like your left arm is stretching. The reverse effect is created by "pushing" the arm back to the starting position. (3) How simple can it be? Since this is an illusion, you will want to practice in front of a mirror until you get the effect you want.

The Old Razzle-Dazzle:

Although this is a very simple ploy, it can be built into quite an amusing gag. I often use it while picking up Eve's toys.

I bend over to pick up a doll and retract my left shoulder slightly, giving the appearance that the doll is just out of my reach. Standing back up, I make a short pull on my arm with my right hand, and again reach for the doll, but it is still just out of the way.

Finally, after several attempts, the task is complete. Eve has become so familiar with this little game that she will often help me stretch my arm to the proper length, just short of dislocating it.

This distraction can also be adapted for the dinner table while reaching for the salt or a glass of milk.

Cashing In

Tricks with Money

It doesn't take a bankroll.
Just some spare change from
your pocket and you're in for
a good time.

Visible Means of Support

How to support a drinking glass on a dollar bill

This is a "betcha" stunt. When I was a little boy, I always used to get caught up in trying to solve puzzles like this one. I also would often find myself doing my brother's chores after losing the bet.

Props: One crisp dollar bill and three small water glasses.

The Old How-To:

(1) Accordion-pleat the dollar bill length-wise.

(2) Place like a bridge across two drinking glasses.

(3) Place the third glass on the bridge and it will be supported.

The Old Razzle-Dazzle:

As I said, this is a "betcha" stunt. You and your little companions can spend some intriguing moments as the problem is set and their imaginations go to work on it.

To set this up, simply ask: "Do you think you can balance this glass on this dollar bill between these two glasses?" Lay the bill flat between the two glasses and poise the third glass above as you ask the question.

"It can be done. Want to give it a try?" On this note, allow your audience to have a go at it. Unless there's a ringer in the crowd, you've got them on the hook.

After they have all tried balancing the glass, you might set up a small wager. "If any of you want to try again, you can have the dollar if you do it. If you can't, I keep the money." This will spark a new enthusiasm but no winners.

Finally, show them how it is done. They are sure to let out a groan, but you can be certain you've stirred the P.T. Barnum in them as they run off looking for their friends to trick and have fun with.

Pulling Out the Carpet

The coke bottle on the dollar trick

In the fine tradition of the "betcha" stunts, I offer yet another one. It actually looks easy until the kids try it, and they are quite surprised when they find the solution is much different from their efforts.

Props: One empty soda bottle and one dollar bill.

The Old How-To:

(1) Invert the bottle and set it on the dollar bill about an inch in from the narrow edge of the bill.

(2) By slowly rolling up the dollar bill toward the bottle, the bill will come out from under the bottle and the bottle will remain balanced.

Note the position of the hands when rolling. They will not bump the bottle but the rolled dollar will.

The Old Razzle-Dazzle:

If the kids were caught in the last one, this "betcha" stunt will seem like a piece of cake to them.

"Okay," you say. "I'm going to give you another chance to win this dollar." Smooth out the bill and put it flat on the table.

"All you have to do is get the dollar from under this bottle without knocking the bottle over." Set the soda bottle upright on the dollar.

"It looks easy, doesn't it? So who's the first to try?" Saying this, turn the bottle over and let the challenge begin. Chances are very good that each of the children will think that a quick snap will win the prize.

When they have all had a shot at the game, simply roll up the bill, smile and put the dollar in your pocket.

Easy Come, Easy Go

How to make a quarter disappear

As a child, I never was any good at guessing which hand "it" was in. No matter how hard I tried, I could never get it right. I figured there had to be some sort of trick to it. You know what? There was!

Props: One quarter.

The Old How-To:

(1) I prefer sitting although you may stand. During a game of "guess which hand," drop the coin on the floor near your right foot. (2) Bend to pick up the coin. But with your fingers masking it, give the coin a push so it shoots under your foot as you complete the motion of picking up the quarter. (3) Continue the game as if you were still holding the coin.

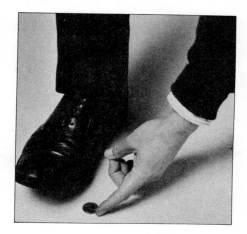

The Old Razzle-Dazzle:

Kids love to have their wits challenged, especially if there is a prize to be won.

Begin by offering a shining coin to the child who can guess which hand you are holding it in. If he guesses correctly the first time, allow him to win. This is the bait.

Extend the offer to another child, this time accidentally dropping the coin. They will think nothing of this as you bend to pick it up.

Of course, there will be no jackpots won no matter how they try. Always keep one hand closed so they will think the coin is in there.

After playing a couple of rounds, tell them, "This was all really a mistake. I only had one quarter and Billy already won it." Open both hands and show that there's no hidden quarter. (Note: You probably should be prepared to give away another quarter to avoid cries of, "That's not fair!"

On Edge

Balancing a coin on a dollar bill

Frankly, betcha tricks always made me feel a little dumb. This one was my secret weapon to get even and stump the stumpers.

Props: One dime and a dollar bill.

The Old How-To:

(1) Fold bill in half, length-wise. Then fold bill end to end. (2) Unfold the bill so it is at a 90° angle and set on table. Place the dime on the corner. (3) Slowly pull ends of the bill in opposite directions. The crease at the middle is enough to support the dime.

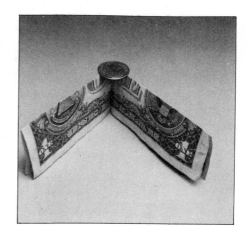

The Old Razzle-Dazzle:

The charm of these puzzles is that the challenge is always taken literally. Of course, from this strategy your money is sure to be safe in your pocket.

The challenge should be made with the dollar bill laid flat. "It takes a steady hand and a good eye to balance things. They say that if you find the right point that you can balance almost anything."

Pick up the dollar bill and hold it stretched out between your hands. "This fellow once told me he could balance a dime on the edge of a dollar bill. I never saw him do it but I guess it can be done. Would you like to give it a try?"

Hand out the dollar and the dime and then sit back and watch as they try their best.

Finally, take back the dollar and make the folds. Place the dime on the corner and slowly pull the bill taut. As with all the betchas I've known, there will be a spontaneous groan. But then groans or giggles all means the same thing — fun.

The Human Piggy-Bank

Rubbing A coin into your arm

Uncle Bob was a frugal man always saving a penny here or a penny there. One day he let us in on a little secret. He began by rolling up his sleeve . . .

Props: One quarter.

The Old How-To:

(1) Roll up the shirt sleeve on your left arm. Bend the arm back so that your hand casually rests at your shirt collar. (2) With right hand rub the quarter up and down on your forearm. Drop the coin. (3) Pick the coin up in your left hand and pretend to pass it to your right hand but keep it in your left. (4) Bend left arm back so that your hand is casually resting at your collar and while repeating the rubbing motions of your right hand, drop the coin down your shirt collar. (5) Slowly move your right hand

away from your arm revealing the coin has vanished.

The Old Razzle-Dazzle:

Like I said, Uncle George was going to let us in on a secret. As he was rolling up his sleeve he would tell us he was going to show us a very special place that he hides his money.

Bending his arm back he'd point to a spot on his arm and say, "Right there. That's where I keep it. Clever isn't it? No one would ever look there." Of course we could see how Uncle George could possibly keep his money there and one of us would ask him to explain what he was talking about.

Smiling he'd explain, "You see, there is a secret opening here, like a slot where I can put coins in. Like this coin." He'd pick up the quarter. Slowly he'd start to rub the coin on his are.

"You've got to be careful and do it slow like this so that you don't make the hole any bigger. Then the money won't always stay in there."

Here he'd drop the coin and pick it right back up with the right hand and begin rubbing again.

"It's the friction that makes the slot open up. Sometimes you have to rub longer than other times." He'd drop the coin again.

He'd then unbend his arm to take a close look at the spot he was rubbing. Actually it was a good reason to be able to pick up the coin in the left hand.

The tricky work done he would go back to rubbing the spot. "Ah, there it goes. Slowly but surely. There."

With this Uncle George would slowly move his hand away showing us the coin was gone.

Rolling his sleeve back down, he'd wink and in a low voice remind us, "It's our secret."

The Almighty Dollar
Breaking a pencil with a dollar bill

This is the childhood stumper that cost me the entire contents of my pencil box one afternoon. I came away with twice as many pencils and puzzled as heck.

Props: One pencil and one crisp dollar bill

The Old How-To:

(1) Have the child grip a long pencil *tightly,* with one hand at the tip and the other at the eraser. (2) Crease a dollar bill lengthwise down the center and grip as shown. (Note how the index finger is curled under.) As you place the bill against the pencil, the child will see there is nothing in the crease. (3) While lifting your hand away from the pencil (blocking the child's view of your grip), slide your index finger into the crease, as shown. (4) Bring the bill down *sharply,* striking the pencil in the center and snapping it in two. As your hand follows through, slide your finger back into the curled position.

The Old Razzle-Dazzle:

Explain that you are about to demonstrate an unusual feat of strength. "Which do you think is stronger, the dollar bill or the pencil?" Wait for the theories. "Well, in fact, this dollar bill can break the pencil clean in two."

Hand the pencil to one of the kids. "Now hold it tight to reinforce it and we'll see which is really the stronger." Usually your assistant will grit his teeth and hold on so tight that his little knuckles will turn white.

"Okay, now hold your arms out in front of you. Here we go!" Touch the bill to the pencil as if lining it up. Actually, hit the pencil so the bill will give. Some kids will sound doubts. Do it again just to reaffirm the doubts.

"Okay, this is it. Hold right!" Pause with the bill resting on the pencil. Now make your move, swiftly bringing the bill down and snapping the pencil clean in two.

The one who will be most surprised will probably be your assistant. I know I was many pencils ago.

Shhhh . . .

Silent Bits

What to do when you have a touch of laryngitis or words just seem to fail you.

Walk A Mile In These!
Making your shoes squeak

I remember a dull party being livened up when an irreverant Uncle Buddy strolled in with this gag, winning squeals of delight from all the kids. Be a star like Buddy and prepare for the giggles.

Props: One long, skinny balloon. Add an oil can if you really want to ham it up.

The Old How-To:

(1) Blow up the balloon part way and twist the end of it, trapping the air in the very end. Let the air out of the rest of the balloon and tie a knot at the twisted place. You can then cut off the excess balloon since the little bubble is all you'll need. (3) Put this in your pocket and slide your thumb over the bubble until you can make a squeak. (4) Here's the tricky part: Walk and squeak the balloon simultaneously.

The Old Razzle-Dazzle:

The key here is timing. Uncle Buddy walked into the room and said hello to everyone. As he crossed the room there was a definite squeaking sound, timed to his steps. He would stop and listen, then walk a little more. More squeaks.

He would then take a step and stop with a squeak. Finally he would look down at his shoes. He would bend his foot and it would squeak.

Some of the kids were already giggling. He would simply say, "New shoes." He would walk a few more steps, squeaking all the way. "Brand new. Gotta break 'em in, I guess." By now the kids were laughing out loud and the grown-ups were chuckling.

That's when Uncle Buddy would clinch it by sitting on the floor, taking an oil can out of his jacket and "oiling" his noisy shoes.

He would put his shoes back on, test them to see if he had gotten all the squeaks out, give a none-too-pleased Aunt Tweet a kiss and off he would go looking for some other trouble to get into. A group of delighted and curious children of course, were trailing behind.

Giving A Leg Up

An elaborate way to cross your legs

Just this side of outrageous, this silent little quickie will never go unnoticed. I use it to break the ice with a little stranger.

← INVISIBLE ROPE

Props: Only your imagination.

The Old How-To:

(1) Walk in a room and sit on a chair or a couch. (2) Pretend to remove a length of rope from your pocket. Take aim and toss it up over an imaginary beam. Tie one end to your knee. (3) Pull the other end, raising your knee in the air as if lifting it. Push knee over the other leg. (4) Lower the rope and the leg as well.

The Old Razzle-Dazzle:

Throwaways like this are good as gold. The best time to try this one out is when all the kids are caught up in some television show and are all quiet.

Make your entrance trying to be as quiet as possible or so it would seem. You might whisper a bit to yourself, trip or whatever, just to let them know you're there.

Take your seat and remove the rope, and tie an end around your knee.

Toss the rope over the beam and begin to pull. Make it an effort and throw in a grunt or two. This is so at least one of them will see what you are doing.

Ask one of the children, in a whisper, to give a hand and hand him the end of the "rope". Together the pulling seems easier.

You might make a sqeaking sound as if an imaginary pulley in need of some oil.

Once you have lifted your leg as high as you need it to clear the other leg have your little helper hold the line tight while you push your hoisted leg into position.

Slowly lower the leg, thank your helper and settle in to watch the television show.

Be sure to reverse the action when you are ready to make your exit.

Flipping Your Lid

Flipping off your hat with style

It was always a treat when-ever Uncle John came to our house for a visit. Meeting him at the door often meant a five-minute routine before you could hang up his hat and coat, but the laughs were well worth the wait.

Props: One hat.

The Old How-To:

(1) Put the hat on your head. With your hands on either side of your head, palms facing in, curl your fingertips just below the hat's rim.

(2) Quickly straighten your fingers, giving the rim a bit of a push. The hat will fly off your head.

The Old Razzle-Dazzle:

Borrowing most of my routine from Uncle John, I begin by explaining, "I was afraid the wind might blow my hat away, so I put it on rather right, and now it doesn't seem to want to come off." I grab the hat by the brim and pretend I'm trying to pull it off my head. No matter how hard I try, it just doesn't budge.

After several unsuccessful attempts I pause, acting a bit winded. Then with a very determined look as if to say, "This had better work or I will have to cut it off," I take a deep breath and hold it, puffing out my cheeks as if building up pressure inside my head.

Placing my hands in position, I screw up my face. Finally, I let the hat go flying with a healthy push of my fingers.

Pop's Losing His Top
Shifting your scalp

Uncle Ray used this gag on us all the time when he came to visit. I could never understand why he never used glue or tape to keep his hair on.

Props: Your own head of hair. Or a toupee, but that's cheating.

The Old How-To:

(1) Wrinkle your forehead. (2) Place hands on either side of your head, thumbs to rear, fingers meeting just below the hairline. (3) All at the same time, move your hands back quickly to the middle of your head, unwrinkle your brow and slightly tilt your head back with a jerk. It will appear you have just shifted the whole top of your head.

The Old Razzle-Dazzle:

After roughhousing, sneezing or coming in from a windy day, this little sight gag can make a big impression.

I like to pretend I have to sneeze, and after the build-up I let go a doozie. Apologizing with an "Oh, dear, excuse me," I rearrange my hair as described. "That one really shook things loose."

For an added touch I tug at my bangs and tilt my head forward with short jerks as if I am straightening the fit.

Egad! Dad Has Lost His Marbles!
The imaginary ball catch

This bit of funny business can solve the problem of playing catch on a rainy day. It requires nothing more than a good imagination and a paper bag, and it's a wonderful way to pass the time with your kids.

Props: One lunch-sized paper sack.

The Old How-To:

(1) Fold down the rim of the bag a couple of times. This will reinforce the sack as well as making it easier to hold. (2) The secret here is the snap. Hold the top back section of the bag in your left hand, with your thumb and second finger outside and the other three fingers inside. (3) Let the children look into the empty bag. (4) Now by snapping or "kicking" the sack with your second finger and dipping the bag slightly, you make the sound and motion of catching something in the bag.

The Old Razzle-Dazzle:

Snap open the bag. "Who wants to play a game of catch?" Reach into the bag as if getting a ball. "Here, Alex, you throw the ball." Hold your hand as if you have a ball in it and pretend to give the ball to Alex.

At first, the kid is probably going to look at you funny. "What's the matter? Don't you see the ball? Come on, use your imagination!" Pretend to toss your imaginary ball high into the air. Watch it fall and catch it in the sack, snapping your fingers as described.

Alex will probably still look at you strangely, but will want to humor you. Hand him the invisible ball again. You can even pretend he dropped it. Point to the ball on the ground and let him use his imagination to pick it up. Then have him toss it to you and you catch it in the bag.

This can be built into a good time for several kids. Pretend to catch all sorts of throws. You can get quite rowdy or keep it quiet. Just keep your timing in mind and you'll have them hooked.

Of course, sometimes you'll want to miss the ball and other times it might arrive in slow motion. It all adds to the fun.

For a surprise finale, have a small rubber ball in your pocket. Get the ball in your hand while no one is looking. When the game is over, reach into the sack and bring out the rubber ball. Give it a bounce on the floor and catch it in the sack.

That will leave them wondering — but at least it will remove the question of your sanity.

Sew What?
Pretending to sew your fingers together

I remember sitting in front of the television with my brothers and watching Red Skelton do this pantomime for the first time. It wasn't long before we were all inventing our own variations and trying to outdo each other.

INVISIBLE THREAD

Props: Your own fingers.

The Old How-To:

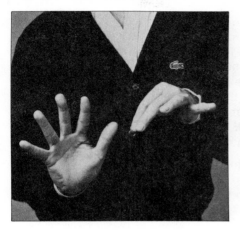 

(1) Pretend to hold a needle in one hand as you use the other hand to pull an imaginary hair from your head or an invisible thread from your clothes. (2) Thread the needle and knot the thread. Remember, this whole gag is a pantomime. Pretend to cut the thread with your teeth like you remember your mother doing. (3) Push the needle through your thumb. (Relax, it won't hurt a bit!) As the imaginary knot reaches your thumb, do a little "tug-o-war" action with the thumb and needle to complete the illusion. (4) Pretend to stick the needle into your next finger and, as it comes out the other side, pull your thumb and finger together. Continue with the other fingers.

The Old Razzle-Dazzle:

Let your imagination go wild with this bit of silliness and it could become ridiculously funny. Take it slow and drag out the action.

Though you're going for the laugh, try to look serious about your sewing. I begin as if I am about to darn socks or something. Many times the kids are not aware that there is no needle or thread until I have "sewn" a couple of fingers together. (Giggling erupts when they catch on.)

Continued . . .

I often use this to amuse curious children in restaurants as they watch me from across the room. I don't even look at them while I sew my fingers together. After I'm done, I look up and smile as I pull the thread down. My fingers bend, then straighten as I release the pull. Gradually, I speed up the motion until I'm waving hello to the curious little stranger. Sometimes they will try imitating my moves, but usually they will look a bit confused — and amused — as they wave back. Maybe they think it's odd that I need a needle and thread to accomplish such a simple task.

The variations with this stunt are limitless. You can sew your fingers and run the thread through your knee to slap your knee in time to the music. Or you can run the thread through your jaw to punch yourself. Or . . .

Face to Face

The Art of Making Funny Mugs

Some faces have launched a thousand ships but you won't find any of them here. No ships, just giggles and laughs.

Face to Face | The art of making funny mugs

I suppose there could be many studies written of the psychology behind the funny face and what makes it so funny, but then, who cares? The fact is that for countless years people have been screwing up their faces for the sole purpose of getting a laugh out of someone.

Harpo Marx, Ben Turpin and the like were masters of the funnyface.

Even my daughter at the age of two understands the potential of changing the shape or expression of the face.

Starting with the basic funny face and with a little inspiration there is no telling what comic genius might evolve.

Following are some old classics that I remember when I was a youngster.

In truth you may not have to go any further in your search for your comic self. This may be just what you've been looking for.

The Basic Face

When it comes to making faces, everyone is a comic. It requires no basic skill or props; just a face and a couple of fingers and you're in business. It's a natural.

* Take two index fingers. Other fingers and quite possibly toes would work here, but we'll keep it simple to start.
* Place the fingers in the corners of your mouth.
* Pull the fingers in opposite horizontal directions, gently but firmly. (A ripped face is very painful.)
* For variety, cross your eyes, stick out your tongue or both.

Junior Birdman

There is a song that goes with this face, leading me to believe it was a product of an early television show. All I really remember is that everyone I grew up with used to do it.

* Form a circle with your thumb and index finger on both hands.
* Extend the other fingers fully.
* Place the "circles" side by side.
* Turn your wrists so that when you place the circles over your face, they form a goggle effect.
* Sing the song.

Just think with this face you can transform just plain old dad into the super hero "The Great Daddo!" defender against boredom and an all around fun guy.

You are on your own on the melody but the words to the song are:

up in the air, Jr. Birdman
up in the air upside down.
up in the air, Jr. Birdman.
with your shoulders to the ground.

Catchy ain't it?

The Beetle or Mosquito

The long, skinny movable nose on this particular face provides a choice opportunity to slip in a tickle or two.

* With your left hand folded so that only the first and second fingers are extended, place the finger tips under each eye.

* Fold the right hand so that only the first finger extends.

* Insert the right finger through the left fingers just below the nose, creating a needle-nose effect.

* Pull the left finger tips down slightly so the eyes sag open a bit.

This is not a very flattering face to say the least however do this in a crowded bus and you'll be sure to have your pick of seats.

What made this face work was the nasal twanging sound you make as the needle nose twitches in search of its next tickle victim.

The Mortimer Snerd

This face is named for one of Edgar Bergen's ventriloquist dummies, Mortimer, who was Charlie McCarthy's sidekick.

* Start as in the basic face, but use your thumbs instead of your index fingers.
* With thumbs in place, put each index finger on the lower eyelids.
* Using a sort of pinching motion, draw your eyelids down and your lip up, creating the effect.

Little really need be said here as the effect itself is quite enough.

You might enhance the overall impression if you were then to talk in a goofy type of voice and laugh like a moron.

Remember this face is to make the children laugh therefore caution should be taken not to do this or any of the other faces while attending an executive board meeting, traffic court, or while having a "discussion" with your spouse (unless no one is looking).

Sad Madelaine

As much as I love to make my little girl giggle, she loves getting even with me and having her share of my laughter. This face is a favorite of hers.

* Place your hands on either side of your face.
* Relax the muscles in your face.
* Now pull your hands downward, causing your features to sag. You'll look pathetic.

I remember when I was a little kid my mother used to yell at us for making faces. "Your face is going to stay like that if you keep it up!"

Now, years on down the line I am actually writing them up in a book. I guess it is safe to say that I didn't fully believe what my mother said about my face sticking that way. At least it hasn't yet.

The Lizard

My Uncle Willy once had an iguana fall madly in love with him when he did this one.

* Draw your head and neck into your shoulders.
* Open your eyes wide and roll them back as far as they'll go.
* Draw your lower lip taut.
* Flick your tongue quickly in and out as any self respecting lizard would do.

This face is particularly charming when you are dressed up in a nice suit or better yet a full tuxedo.

Occasionally dart the tongue way out and back with a slurp as if snaring a fly. Perfectly charming!

Fish Face

Not only silly but this face is great for stealing fish kisses.

* Suck in your cheeks.
* Don't stop. Keep sucking them in until there is nothing left but a little guppy mouth.
* Open your eyes real wide then cross them.
* Now move your lips a la goldfish.

Once on a field trip to an aquarium I convinced my school chums that you could actually talk to the fish in this manner. What a sight to see six fish faced children all in a row.

Windshield Wipers

This face can be the first step to turning a gloomy, rainy day into one filled with lots of fun and laughter.

* Lace your fingers together with the fingers to the backs of your hands.
* From this position move your second fingers on both hands to the palm side.
* Hold your hands to your forehead like a visor.
* Now by bending and unbending your fingers you create the wiper effect.

Of course, this little bit is not going to be of much help to you in a regular downpour but they work just like the real things.

By varying speeds you are as well equipped as you can be in light to heavy rain, even a slight mist.